AWFUL ANIMALS

by
Charis Mather

BEARPORT PUBLISHING

Minneapolis, Minnesota

Credits

Images are courtesy of Shutterstock.com. With thanks to GettyImages, ThinkstockPhoto, and iStockphoto.

Cover – Vector_Up, irin-k, Eric Isslee. Recurring images – gravity_point, yugoro, The_Pixel, lyeyee, Voin_Sveta, nataliiudina, ozzichka, johnjohnson. 2–3 – Sorbis. 4–5 – Eric Isselee, VP Photo Studio. 6–7 – Ethan Daniels, Laura Dts. 8–9 – Francisco Blanco, Svetlana Foote. 10–11 – aaltair, frank60, photowind. 12–13 – Emőke Dénes (Wikimedia Commons), Jose Barquero. J, Paul Starosta. 14–15 – Jesus Cobaleda, Nick Pecker. 16–17 – Agnieszka Bacal, Debbie Steinhausser, Anna Violet. 18–19 – Agami Photo Agency, John Navajo, Vishnevskiy Vasily. 20–21 – Chanasid kaewpirun, Novim images. 22–23 – Keri Delaney, Rob Hainer.

Library of Congress Cataloging-in-Publication Data

Names: Mather, Charis, 1999- author.
Title: Awful animals / by Charis Mather.
Description: Minneapolis, Minnesota : Bearport Publishing Company, [2024] | Series: Beastly wildlife | Includes index.
Identifiers: LCCN 2023031104 (print) | LCCN 2023031105 (ebook) | ISBN 9798889163381 (library binding) | ISBN 9798889163435 (paperback) | ISBN 9798889163473 (ebook)
Subjects: LCSH: Animals--Juvenile literature.
Classification: LCC QL49 .M4325 2024 (print) | LCC QL49 (ebook) | DDC 590--dc23/eng/20230713
LC record available at https://lccn.loc.gov/2023031104
LC ebook record available at https://lccn.loc.gov/2023031105

For more information, write to Bearport Publishing, 5357 Penn Avenue South, Minneapolis, MN 55419.

CONTENTS

BEASTLY!

Animals can be amazing, but some can be pretty awful, too. Check out these animals that are nasty, mean, and just downright beastly.

WHAT'S THAT SUPPOSED TO MEAN?!

As cool as some of these **creatures** look, you might not want to get too close. These awful animals are probably best enjoyed from far, far away!

STRANGE SEA CUCUMBERS

Believe it or not, sea cucumbers aren't vegetables. They are long, skinny sea creatures with **tentacle**-like parts along their bodies. They use some of these sticky tentacles, called tube feet, to push food into their mouths.

But sticky tube feet are not the weirdest thing about them. These crazy creatures can shoot their own guts out of their bodies . . . and grow them back later! Wow!
Guts
Sea cucumbers shoot out their guts to confuse other animals that try to eat them.

GREEDY GATORS

When you are really hungry, you might feel like you could eat just about anything. Well, alligators really will. If they get hungry enough, these beastly creatures will even chow down on other gators. *Yikes!*

Alligators use their powerful jaws to chomp down on a meal. Any creatures that find themselves near alligators have to be very careful.

UNLOVABLE LEECHES

Leeches may look harmless, but don't be fooled. Many of these worms drink blood. *Yum!*

Leeches use suckers to stick themselves to other creatures.

SLURP!

It can be difficult to know if you've been bitten by a leech unless you see it on you. The leech's **saliva** makes its bite feel less painful. Once it's on you, a leech can drink about 10 times its own weight in blood!

HAIRY HORROR FROGS

If you think slimy frogs are gross, wait until you see hairy horror frogs. They look like they have hair on their backs, but in reality the hairs are many bits of skin.

Hairy frogs are even creepier when they are in danger. These frogs can pop out some of the bones in their feet to **protect** themselves. *Crack!* The bones break through the skin to become sharp claws.

FOUL FULMARS

Fulmars are seabirds. They have a surprising trick to keep unwanted visitors away. The birds **vomit** an oily spray from their stomachs to shoot at their enemies.

Other birds that attack fulmars have to be careful. If this smelly vomit gets on the enemies' wings, it can make flying almost impossible.

Skunks may look cute and fluffy, but if you see one, beware. Skunks have a stinky secret weapon. They shoot a smelly **musk** from under their tails. It can reach a target more than 10 feet (3 m) away.

ME? SPRAY STINK? NEVER!

Skunks usually give plenty of warning before they spray. They might stomp their feet and lift their tails. After that, anyone who gets close will probably smell awful for days. *Pee-yew!*

Some skunks do a warning handstand before they make a stink.

CRUEL CUCKOOS

Many cuckoo birds lay their eggs in other birds' nests. This tricks the other birds into caring for young cuckoo chicks. Cuckoos even push some of the other eggs out of the nest to make space for their babies.

Watch out! Cuckoo chicks aren't any nicer than their mothers. When they **hatch**, baby cuckoos beg for food the loudest to try to get the most to eat.

FILTHY FLIES

When it comes to food, flies are not picky. They will eat many things that we find disgusting. Flies happily snack on rotting food, dead animals, and even poop.

Before chowing down, flies spit on their food. Their saliva helps turn it into a wet sludge. Once the food is good and soupy, flies slurp it all up. Imagine drinking a puddle of spit. . . . *Yuck!*

Some animals have weird ways of protecting themselves. Others have foul taste in food. And some animals . . . well, they just stink.

JUST HOW I LIKE IT!

Whatever you think about these awful animals, the truth is that the world would be pretty boring without them. Wildlife can be beastly. But sometimes, beastly is best!

GLOSSARY

creatures animals

hatch to break out of an egg

musk an oil that has a strong smell

protect to keep safe from harm

saliva liquid in the mouth that helps with eating

tentacle a long, thin body part on some animals that is used for moving, feeling, or grasping

vomit to throw up

INDEX